THE VICTORY

by

DUMITRU STANILOAE

INTRODUCTION BY

A. M. ALLCHIN

SLG PRESS
Convent of the Incarnation
Fairacres   Oxford
0X4 1TB

© THE SISTERS OF THE LOVE OF GOD 1970

Ninth Impression 1991

ISBN 0 7283 0049 4
ISSN 0307-1405

ACKNOWLEDGEMENT

With the exception of the last quotation from Job (42:1ff), and the passage from the Song of Songs, which are taken from the *Authorised Version*, the *New English Bible* has been used with permission from the Oxford and Cambridge University Presses.

INTRODUCTION

During his visit to England during the summer of 1970, Fr. Dumitru Staniloae was able to spend some days in Oxford, staying at the Convent of the Incarnation, Fairacres. On the last morning of his stay he spoke to the whole Community on the meaning of the cross. The following article has been made from the recording of what he said then, supplemented by further explanations provided by Fr. Staniloae. The subject had arisen out of a discussion on the meaning of suffering, and in particular of undeserved suffering. Here as always the teaching of this theologian arises out of experience and illuminates experience. Romania was one of the countries which in the course of 1970 suffered a catastrophic natural disaster in the form of devastating floods. But the experience which lies behind the following pages is not, of course, only the experience of a single moment or event. What is written here comes from a lifetime lived in solidarity with the sufferings of mankind, in a century when the peoples of Europe have suffered two world wars and all that has followed from them. It comes from the centuries' old experience of the Church as it has learned to live in the dying and rising of the Lord. There is here a combination of great simplicity and directness with profound perception and understanding. Learning and life have come together into one.

Father Dumitru Staniloae is Professor of Dogmatic Theology in the Theological Institute of Bucharest. He is also the editor of the Romanian version of the *Philokalia*. He is therefore equally familiar with the realms of theology and spirituality. Himself a married priest, he is well known and well loved in the monasteries and convents of Romania. He prefaced his talk at Fairacres with some remarks about the monastic life, speaking of the Eastern icon which depicts the monk as crucified. All men find the cross in their lives. The monk is one who accepts it willingly and can therefore find joy through it, the joy of Christ who took up the cross in freedom and in love. 'One sees in the faces of monks and nuns everywhere a joy and a serenity . . . It is the sign of their victory over the weakness of their humanity through their union with Christ. I see this joy here too. Jesus "had no man" with him, either in Gethsemane or on the cross. In Gethsemane the apostles were asleep. On Calvary all had abandoned him. We have Christ with us. He does not sleep and he has not fled. It is he who gives us the victory and the joy in our cross, and this joy is the foretaste of the resurrection'.

The morning of September 2nd when this talk was given was in many ways a memorable one for those who were present, not least because of the depth of unity which was revealed in the discussion which followed it. The life and prayer of the SLG Community has been, and is, deeply indebted to the teaching of the great Carmelite saints of sixteenth-century Spain, St Teresa and St John of the Cross. Though the Sisters of the Love of God have never claimed to be Carmelites in the strict sense of the word, the tradition of Carmel has been fundamental to the whole development of their life. It is commonly said, even by writers of real authority, that the teaching of St John of the Cross about the 'dark nights' through which man must pass on the journey into the love and knowledge of God, have no counterpart in Eastern Christendom. But the Community at once recognised in the teaching of the latter part of Fr Staniloae's address, a thought and an experience identical with that which is conveyed in the works of St John of the Cross by the image of the nights of sense and spirit. The darkness, the night, these are images to describe the ways which lead towards the union of love and glory, ways by which God himself becomes active to take man beyond all created things into union with himself, the uncreated Giver of all. Only through the cross do we arrive at the resurrection.

But this was not all, for a Franciscan friend who happened to be present exclaimed that the talk of Fr Staniloae had given him a new and deeper understanding of his own father in the faith, St Francis. It had shown him how it was that the different elements in the life of St Francis, love for the creation, fervent devotion to the cross, and overflowing joy in the resurrection, were inseparably united. The teaching of St Maximus the Confessor, one of the greatest but least known of the Eastern fathers, which lies behind much of the thought of Fr Staniloae, in this way illuminates the life of the most loved of Western saints, and shows how the different sides of his character form a single whole. The universal, cosmic vision of Orthodox faith reveals the true meaning of St Francis' love for the created world.

It seems that here we can see not only something of the unifying power of the Orthodox tradition at its deepest and best, but also something of the way in which the ecumenical dialogue between the Churches must be carried on. The questions of dogmatic theology cannot and must not be avoided. But they need to be met at the place where theology and spirituality come together into one. When they are seen in relation to the living and praying experience of the Christian people, then we find unexpected possibilities of reconciliation between positions which appear at first sight to be absolutely opposed. Where the mind is being re-established in the heart, where man's different faculties are coming into union as they do in prayer, there understanding and deep agreement becomes possible. *Cor ad cor loquitur.* This is why monasteries and convents and all places where prayer is made have such great potential significance in the work of Christian unity.

Nothing could illustrate the truth of this last assertion better than to quote the remarks which Fr. Staniloae added after the end of his address. Despite all difficulties of language, he had found himself at once at home, his message had received an instant recognition. With their warmth and humour these words convey better than anything else could something of the atmosphere of the occasion:

'In the Eastern Church, monasteries have the custom of giving hospitality to people for three days. There is a story of someone who stayed for the fourth day and could not find the towel when he wanted to dry his face in the morning. He called the guest-master and said, "Why haven't I got a towel?" "What do you need a towel for?" enquired the guest-master. "To dry my face!" replied the visitor. "Oh? Have you still got any face?"

Dear Sisters in Christ, I have stayed more than three days here, and I have found not only a towel, but also a love and care which goes beyond anything I could imagine. I have found a family here, and all the warmth and love of a family, a spiritual family in which I have found a complete convergence of thought and desire with that of my own heart and mind. I thank you for all this harmony of spirit. May God give you the power to carry the cross of renunciation and service for the salvation of men, the continual renewal of your Church, and for the unity of all the Churches'.

A.M. Allchin
February 1971

THE VICTORY OF THE CROSS

The cross imprinted on the gift of the world

The world is a gift of God, but the destiny of this gift is to unite man with God who has given it. The intention of the gift is that in itself it should be continually transcended. When we receive a gift from somebody we should look primarily towards the person who has given it and not keep our eyes fixed on the gift. But often the person who receives a gift becomes so attached to the gift that he forgets who has given it to him. But God demands an unconditional love from us for he is infinitely greater than any of the gifts which he gives us; just as at the human level the person who gives us a gift is incomparably more important than the gift which he has given and should be loved for himself and not only on account of his gift. In this way every gift requires a certain cross, and this cross is meant to show us that all these gifts are not the last and final reality. This cross consists in an alteration in the gift, and sometimes even in its entire loss.

We can see many meanings in this cross which is imprinted on the gift of the world which God gives to us. St. Maximus the Confessor said that 'all the realities which we perceive with the senses demand the cross'; and 'all the realities which we understand with our mind have need of the tomb'. To these words of St. Maximus we can add this: that man in his fallen condition feels the dissolution of the present world and of his own existence as a pain, a suffering; feels it as a sorrow because he has bound the affections which form part of his very being to the image of this world which is passing away. This attachment to the things of this world is felt particularly strongly by those who do not believe that there is any further transformation of this world after the life which we now know.

The Christian, however, carries this cross of the world and of his own existence not only more easily but with a certain joy, for he knows that after this cross there follows an imperishable life. With this faith he sees the world as crucified and dead to him, and he and all his tendencies as crucified and dead to the present world. This does not mean that he is not active in this world, and that he does not exercise his responsibility towards it; but he works in order to develop in the present state of the world, destined as it is to dissolution and death, the germs, the seeds of its future resurrection. He longs that this world, and his own existence in it, may be crucified as Christ was crucified; that is to say he wishes voluntarily to undergo the suffering of the cross with the hope of resurrection into a higher world, an imperishable world, a resurrection which is truly with and in Christ.

The Christian does not see the transitory nature of the structures of this world and of his own existence as leading towards a crucifixion without hope, or as moving towards a definitive, final death. He sees this situation and he lives it, anticipating the crucifixion at its end with hope, the hope of a higher and unchanging life.

However, it is not only the Christian who lives his own life and that of the world in anticipation of their crucifixion, lives them as nailed to the cross of the passing away of their present form; everyone inevitably does so. For everyone knows that those we love will die, and this certainty introduces a sorrow into the joy of our communion with them. Everyone knows that the material goods which one accumulates are transitory, and this knowledge casts a shadow on the pleasure one has in them. In this sense, the world and our own existence in it are a cross which we shall carry until the end of our earthly life. Never can man rejoice wholly in the gifts, the good things, and in the persons of this world. We feel the transitory nature of this world as a continual cross. But Christians can live this cross with the hope of the resurrection, and thus with joy, while those who have no faith must live this experience with increasing sadness, with the feeling that existence is without meaning, and with a certain despair which they cannot altogether alleviate.

The cross in relationships

Our responsibility towards those who are near to us forms the weight of a particularly heavy and painful cross on account of the fragility of their life which is exposed to a multitude of ills, a multitude of difficulties which arise from the conditions of this world in its present state. Parents suffer intensely and very frequently because of the ills and difficulties of their children; they fear for their life, for their failure, for their sufferings. Therefore the life of parents becomes a life of continual concern, and the cross of the children is their cross. Our cross becomes heavier with the weight of the cross of those with whom we come in contact, for we share responsibility for the life of our children, our relatives, our friends, and even of all men with whom, in one way and another, we are in touch. We bear responsibility for all that can threaten the life of those for whom we have care, and we have the obligation, so far as we can, of smoothing their difficulties and helping their lives. Thus we can reveal and strengthen our love for them and their love for us; thus we can develop the seeds of a future life in strengthening our and their spiritual existence. In this responsibility towards our neighbour we live more intensely our responsibility towards God. Christ has shown this meaning of his cross, he who had pity on those who were suffering, and wept for those who were dead.

A second sense of the cross in relationships is this: The fallen world is often lived and felt as a cross to be carried until death through the fact that people sometimes act towards us in a hostile way, even though we have done them no wrong. They suspect us of having evil intentions towards them. They think of us as obstacles in the path of their life. Often they become our enemies even on account of the noble and high convictions to which we remain faithful. Our attachment to these convictions brings their evil designs into the light and their bad intentions to view even though we do not intend this. And this happens all the more because by the beliefs which we hold, and which we cannot renounce, we show our responsibility towards them, since we seek the security of their physical and material life and the true development of their spiritual being. This is a responsibility which we reveal in our words, our writings and our actions which become, as it were, an exhortation to them.

We also feel as a heavy cross the erring ways of our children, of our brethren, and of many of our neighbours and contemporaries. We carry their incomprehension of our good intentions and of our good works as a cross. Almost every one of our efforts to spread goodness is accompanied by suffering and by a cross which we carry on account of the incomprehension of others. To wish to avoid this suffering, this cross, would mean in general to renounce the struggle and the effort to do what is good. Thus without the cross there can be no true growth and no true strengthening of the spiritual life. To avoid the weight of this cross is to avoid our responsibility towards our brethren and our neighbours before God. Only by the cross can we remain in submission to God and in true love towards our neighbours. We cannot purify or develop our own spiritual life, nor that of others, nor that of the world in general, by seeking to avoid the cross. Consequently, we do not discover either the depth or the greatness of the potential forces and powers of this world as a gift of God if we try to live without the cross. The way of the cross is the only way which leads us upwards, the only way which carries creation towards the true heights for which it was made. This is the signification which we understand of the cross of Christ.

The cross in innocence and in guilt

The third point is this. None of us find ourselves in the situation of Christ, a situation of total purity, having the unique capacity of carrying the cross without any personal sin. Only Christ knew this condition; only in him is the cross truly the power of God, as St. Paul says. (1 Cor. 1:18) In him alone it has the power of rooting evil out at its roots. With us purity is always mixed with impurity, innocence with guilt, and the cross comes to us in great part because of our fault, because of our sin and the presence of impurity within the purity which God gives us; it also comes to us through the responsibility with which we fight on behalf of our neighbours in order to bring them also to truer beliefs. And we suffer in the struggle for our own growth in perfection, while Christ suffered exclusively for others, for their perfection and for their salvation.

The cross which Christ carried in perfect purity and innocence is unjust, and it cannot have the last word. The cross we carry for our sinfulness is just, and is all the more just the greater is our sinfulness. Our cross can be lightened by the power of the cross of Christ who carried it being totally pure and innocent; and it is he who will raise us up, if we do not remain rooted in our own wickedness.

The total purity and innocence of Christ is full of an overwhelming power which is revealed in the fact that Christ carried the cross for love of mankind and not at all in order to overcome or to root out any evil within himself. Because there was no evil in Christ, therefore, the power of his cross and the strength of his love can spread itself to all men who are willing to open their hearts to Christ who suffers for them. St. Maximus the Confessor says, 'He who suffers death on account of his sins, suffers justly. But he who does not suffer on account of sin, voluntarily accepts death, which was introduced into the world on account of sin, and thus overcomes sin and, by the divine dispensation, grants a grace to all human nature by which it overcomes sin'. *(Quaest. ad Thal. 22,* Migne *P.G. 90)*

The power which comes from suffering even to death was added in Christ to the power of the total purity of his human nature, or rather, it is to be understood by this purity, which itself contains the supreme human power of love. It gives to the human nature which the Son of God assumed, the power to overcome death in him and through him. In him and through him this power is communicated to the human nature of all those who are united with Christ; in them it overcomes sin and consequently it overcomes death. For sin means egotism; and love, the pure love of Christ, surpasses and destroys all egotism—all selfishness.

Of the two thieves who were crucified with Christ one said, 'It is just that we should be thus condemned to death for we receive the payment of our transgressions, but this man has done nothing evil'. These words tell us that there is no one except Christ who is not obliged to carry his cross with a certain justice and on account of a certain culpability. If our neighbours suspect our thoughts and intentions, it is almost always true that our thoughts towards them, or towards others, have not been filled with perfect love. If they criticise us it is because we have not always helped them in their own difficult circumstances. It is almost always certain that we have not given them all the help that we could have done, and have not opened our heart to them. If they forget the help which we have given them it is because we ourselves do not fully rejoice in the good things which have come to them because of the help which we have been able to give. If a tension or coldness exists between me and another person, it is almost certain that I am at least in part the cause of this tension or coldness, or at least that I have not done all that I could to get rid of it. Bad relationships between myself and other people nearly always have their roots in me as well as in the others. I ought to support the hostility of other people not only as a cross which I bear for myself but as a cross which I bear for them as well, since I carry this cross because, on account of the kind of person I am, they are not able to be in the relationship with me which they would wish to be. Every cross which has saving power is a cross which I carry not only on account of my own sins, but also on account of the sins of others. I should bend and bow in carrying my neighbour with his cross, and in bowing and bending I spiritually form the horizontal line, the humbling line of the cross, in order that the one whom I carry may form the vertical line as I carry him on my shoulders. Our moral weakness and powerlessness, our insufficient responsibility towards God and our neighbours, these form our cross.

So just as the man who will not accept his responsibility for others will not accept the human condition—the true condition of man—so the man who recognises himself as guilty towards others never fails to become truly human. For he who recognises himself as guilty recognises his own personal responsibility and his insufficiency in working it out, while he who does not recognise himself as guilty cannot recognise himself as responsible. Such a man in his actions does not respond to God, and he refuses to admit that he has not replied as he should in the past to God and to others. For it is certain that because of our human condition after the fall, we have not replied fully and satisfactorily either to God or to our neighbour. In our recognition of our fault we begin to live our true personal relationship of dialogue with God. But if we do not recognise our fault then implicitly we do not recognise our responsibility. In this way man shows that he refuses the role of a responsible partner in the dialogue of relationship with God, and that he no longer acknowledges God as the one who addresses a word to him and who calls for his reply.

In refusing this relationship with God, man falls altogether out of the human condition, for the true human condition consists in our ability to hear the word of God, to enter into personal relationship with God, And, consequently, he also loses the ability of hearing his neighbour's word to him, and of entering into true relationship with him. He falls from reality into a shadowy, pseudo-reality, into outer darkness. And here we find another suffering, another cross, but this is an unwilling cross, a cross without hope. The selfish, egotistic person suffers much more than the one who wishes to help others. In refusing relationship with others we jump out of reality, for the reality of the world and of our own person can only be truly and fully lived when we are aware of our responsibility and of our fault, and are willing to carry our cross for others.

The cross in pain and pleasure

St. Maximus the Confessor also speaks of another kind of suffering. He speaks of the pain which follows upon pleasure. Every indulgence of pleasure brings a pain, a sorrow in its wake. Both the pain and the pleasure represent an excessive sensibility, or capacity for feeling, on the part of the body and the flesh, and consequently there is a close relationship between them. Strictly speaking however, pleasure leads to pain, but pain does not lead to pleasure. Indulgence in pleasure only pushes a man into a further attempt to escape from pain in further pleasure. While man by his will can renounce pleasure, he can never wholly avoid pain and sorrow. He can only overcome his sorrow, that is to say, remain in it, carrying his cross, without taking refuge in a new pleasure which would bring with it a new pain, and so on till at the end of his life, death will come as the final sorrow. Christ overcame pleasure, that is to say, the human tendency towards pleasure, by remaining in grief, victoriously bearing the cross, as the ultimate pain. *(Quaest. ad Thal. 22,* Migne *P.G. 90)* In this way he freed human nature from the domination of an excessive sensibility, an unbalanced power of feeling, and re-established the power of the spirit. For he did not overcome pleasure and pain by a sort of stoic insensibility, an inability to feel; he mastered them through the strengthening of his spirit, thus at the same time preserving yet transfiguring our full human sensibility to suffering and our tendency to want to escape from it.

His cross means that the spirit is victorious over matter without making matter of no effect, but by transfiguring the material world through the response of a will wholly given to God. We can see this in the very form of the human body: we stretch out our hands towards nature to master it, and do not passively leave it as it is, but our head is raised above the horizontal level and is held high. The cross prevents the base tendencies of the world and of the human body from being raised up like a tower of Babel; but it also gives them the possibility of being transfigured by passing through the horizontal line of the cross which purifies them. In the Orthodox office of burial we sing 'Death came in order that the evil of man should not be without end'. The same is true in some measure of every suffering.

St. Maximus the Confessor speaks to us of a blind pleasure, a pleasure from which the vision of the spirit is absent, a pleasure which does not look either towards our responsibility to God, or to our neighbour. A pleasure in which this spiritual vision was present, even if it was in part a bodily pleasure, would not inevitably bring sorrow and a cross with it as a consequence. But in his fallen condition it is only with difficulty that man can feel in his body pleasures of this kind, pleasures which are enlightened by the life of the spirit of God, and by a sense of responsibility towards our neighbours. All his pleasures tend to be blind pleasures. They do not look beyond themselves. They are excessively egotistical and carnal. Through them man falls into sensations without any horizon. He falls into the darkness of an ego which is reduced to the sensations which are produced by the material world which thus becomes heavy and no longer transparent to greater realities. Consequently the sorrow felt after such pleasure brings with it a spiritual feeling of weakness and of disorder in the material aspect of human life. This is the result of an abuse of pleasure. The pain which follows on from pleasure is a reflection of the weakening of matter in the spiritual realm, and in this sense it can be understood as a manifestation of the spirit. Grief, or the cross, make the spirit transparent in matter, or make matter transparent for the spirit. In this way sorrow becomes transfiguring and prophetic. It shows us that the material world, and the feelings of pleasure produced by it, are not a final reality but that beyond them there is a life of the spirit lived in and through matter transfigured by spirit. The cross points us to the resurrection, and to the way which leads to the resurrection. The Fathers say that he who is nourished by the cross is nourished by the tree of life. By the cross the world and our own life become transparent.

However, one cannot say that every sorrow is of itself the sign of the spirit, the indication of a future and better life. Only those sorrows which are borne without rebelling against them, that is to say with an understanding of their meaning, have this quality. The revelation of the spirit is not produced by suffering alone, but by the understanding which it can awaken in the spirit. If man refuses to open the eyes of his spirit, refuses to see what is beyond the material world, and continues to think of himself as exclusively identified with the material world, then the cross of suffering can be of no profit to him. Finally, such a man being without hope, and in the course of time losing the very possibility of escaping into selfish and material pleasures, which at least give him some feeling of being alive, must sink into darkness and despair over the total non-sense of life. Such a one is lost by the cross for eternity. St. Augustine said: *Cognosco tres homines, unum qui per crucem salvat, alterum qui per crucem salvatur, et alterum qui per crucem damnatur.* 'I know three men. By the cross one saves, by the cross another is saved, by the cross the third is condemned'. Only Christ belongs to the first category. We, all other men, belong to the other two.

No one can escape the cross on this earth. But he who wishes to avoid it, he who does not see or does not wish to see God through it, will be lost by it. He who seeks to separate the gift of the world, the gift of life, from the cross, never really succeeds in doing so. He finally loses the gift itself because he does not see it as the gift of God who reveals his own reality as greater than the gift, and who shows the way towards himself by the cross. He remains definitively weighed down under the weight of his suffering, that is in hell. The cross is given to all of us to lead us towards the life of the spirit and as a means of re-establishing the dialogue of man with God. It is given to all because in it the meaning of life is objectively to be found. But the one who does not discover this meaning in it will be totally lost in the darkness which his suffering causes him, since his suffering instead of revealing the meaning will hide it more impenetrably.

The cross and Job's quest for its meaning

If the function of the cross is to reveal God as the one who transcends all his gifts, the cross can also be given to the man who is relatively righteous—and then it accomplishes its full function.

We have said that after the fall the cross has a sense of expiation for all men because there is no man who is totally innocent. But we must always recognise that often the weight of the cross which men have to carry is not proportional to their sins. This situation has made many men speak of the mystery of suffering because very often those who are relatively righteous seem to have a heavy share of suffering.

The theme of this mystery is discussed in the book of Job. Job wished to know the cause of his suffering, he wished to see beyond the cross which had been given to him, to the faults of his past so that he might understand the meaning of his cross. Job does not pretend not to have committed sin. But on the other hand he is not content with imprecise and sentimental generalisations, simply saying that because no man is without sin therefore he must be a great sinner, and that it is on account of his sins that his great sufferings have come to him. But, as one who thinks out the problem soberly and thoroughly, he wants to go further. He sees that his sufferings are not equivalent to his faults because his sins are not as great as those of many other men who suffer much less than he does. Job asks God:

> *How many iniquities and sins are laid to my charge?*
> *Let me know my offences and my sin.*
> *Why dost thou hide thy face*
> *and treat me as thy enemy?*

(13:23-24)

And:

> *I will say to God, 'Do not condemn me,*
> *but tell me the ground of thy complaint against me...'*

(10:2-3)

Job does not agree with those who see the cause of suffering as being *always* in the unrighteousness of those who suffer and say therefore that the cause of Job's suffering is simply his lack of righteousness. And God also disagrees with them! So Job rejects the views of Eliphaz when Eliphaz

says:
> *What makes you so bold at heart,*
> *and why do your eyes flash,*
> *that you vent your anger on God*
> *and pour out such a torrent of words?*
> *What is frail man that he should be innocent,*
> *or any child of woman that he should be justified?*
> *If God puts no trust in his holy ones,*
> *and the heavens are not innocent in his sight,*
> *how much less so is man, who is loathsome and rotten*
> *and laps up evil like water!*
>
> *I will tell you, if only you will listen,*
> *and I will describe what I have seen . . .*
> *the wicked are racked with anxiety all their days,*
> *the ruthless man for all the years in store for him.*
> *The noise of the hunter's scare rings in his ears,*
> *and in time of peace the raider falls on him;*
> *he cannot hope to escape from dark death;*
> *he is marked down for the sword;*
> *he is flung out as food for vultures;*
> *such a man knows that his destruction is certain.*
> *Suddenly a black day comes upon him . . .*
> *for he has lifted his hand against God*
> *and is pitting himself against the Almighty . . .*

(15:12-17;20-25)

He again disagrees with Elihu when Elihu says:
> *Take care not to turn to mischief;*
> *for that is why you are tried by afflictions.*

(36:21)

But at the same time Job recognises God's right to send sufferings to him and does not give way to his wife's encouragement to blaspheme against God because he has sent him suffering although he has done no wrong. God has the right to give his gifts and to withdraw them. And man should not make his attachment to God conditional on the gifts which God has given. Such an attitude would not be a true love for God but an attachment to the gifts in themselves, and this would mean to put the gifts above the giver. In this case the relationship of man with God would simply be founded on a contract and man would say, 'I shall remain devoted to you as long as you give me things'. Such an attitude on man's part would mean that God was not worthy of being loved for himself. Man's relationship with God in such a case would depend on the usefulness which man has from the gifts which God gives him. And then man would really be loving himself. In this way the gifts would lose their meaning as signs of God's love and as the means by which man enters into and maintains a personal relationship with God. The gifts would become just things in themselves. The point of view of Job's wife is basically the same as the point of view of Job's friends who say that God gives things to those who remain faithful to him and takes away his gifts when they become unfaithful. They say essentially the same thing because both affirm that man remains faithful to God on account of his gifts and that these gifts are an inevitable payment which God returns to man as a reward for his faithfulness to him.

It is to this view that Job owes all his sufferings for it is propounded to God by Satan at the beginning of the book when he claims that Job loves God simply because he has given him great riches and that he would not love God if he took away his gifts. Satan is a cynic and says that man loves God merely for the gifts and objects which God gives him. Satan cannot conceive that a man could love God for himself, that through love man could transcend himself and his own circle of interests. But God wishes to show by the example of Job that there is such a love, that man is capable of remaining attached to God himself even if he no longer receives his gifts. In order to show this, God sometimes breaks the close link which exists between the just man and the gifts which God gives him. This is how it is in the case of Job: the gifts which God gives to someone may not be the inevitable consequence of his faithfulness towards God.

Job sees this but he is not able to understand why it is that God sometimes breaks this link between his gifts and himself. He sees that God is pursuing him with moral and material blows and evils, and he does not deny God's right to do this. Through his sufferings he understands that God is showing an interest and concern for him, but he does not understand what kind of an interest or concern it is on God's part that is being shown him:

> *God has left me at the mercy of malefactors*
> *and cast me into the clutches of wicked men.*
> *I was at ease, but he set upon me and mauled me,*

> *seized me by the neck and worried me.*
> *He set me up as his target;*
> *his arrows rained upon me from every side;*
> *pitiless, he cut deep into my vitals,*
> *he spilt my gall on the ground.*
> *He made breach after breach in my defences;*
> *he fell upon me like a fighting man.*
>
> *I stitched sackcloth together to cover my body*
> *and I buried my forelock in the dust;*
> *my cheeks were flushed with weeping*
> *and dark shadows were round my eyes,*
> *yet my hands were free from violence*
> *and my prayer was sincere.*
>
> (16:11-17)

And in an earlier chapter he declares:
> *I would rather be choked outright;*
> *I would prefer death to all my sufferings.*
> *I am in despair, I would not go on living*
> *leave me alone, for my life is but a vapour.*
> *What is man that thou makest much of him*
> *and turnest thy thoughts towards him,*
> *only to punish him morning by morning*
> *or to test him every hour of the day?*
> *Wilt thou not look away from me for an instant?*
> *Wilt thou not let me be while I swallow my spittle?*
> *If I have sinned, how do I injure thee,*
> *thou watcher of the hearts of men?*
> *Why hast thou made me thy butt,*
> *and why have I become thy target?*
> *Why dost thou not pardon my offence*
> *and take away my guilt?*
>
> (7:15-20)

The cross and God's revelation of its meaning

In the end it is God alone who can explain the sufferings of the righteous, and he does it through the many questions which he asks Job, all of which draw Job's attention to the Giver of gifts. God in effect says to Job, 'All my gifts are wonderful, but the intention of their wonder is to reveal the infinite wisdom and greatness of the one who gives them all'.

> Then Job answered the Lord and said:
> I know that thou canst do every thing,
> and that no thought can be withheld from thee . . .
> I have uttered that I understood not;
> things too wonderful for me, which I knew not . . .
> I have heard of thee by the hearing of the ear;
> but now mine eye seeth thee.
> Wherefore I abhor myself,
> and repent in dust and ashes.
>
> (42:1-3;5-6)

This means to say that up until this moment Job had always thought of God in much the same terms in which others had spoken of him; now he begins to understand God himself, beyond all his gifts, the Giver of everything. In order to gain this supreme treasure he had for a while to lose all his possessions. He lost the respect of others, he lost his health, his wealth—all things—in order to see God in all his greatness and wisdom and marvellous nature. In losing all things he did not doubt God and thus he came to see the apophatic, inexpressible character of God who is beyond all human understanding. He saw God in a higher way than is possible merely through his gifts. He saw him immediately through his suffering.

The believer continually needs to make abstraction of the things of this world, needs to put the things of this world into brackets of forgetfulness, in order to think of God who is above all human understanding. But sometimes it is necessary that God himself should intervene in order to throw into relief the little value of the things of this world in comparison with God, their transitory, passing nature in contrast to the eternity of God, in order to show us more clearly God's infinite transcendence of his gifts and his ineffable presence with us. In such cases it seems to us that God himself abandons us. This is because sometimes we become so attached to things that we can no longer see God. Sometimes we make so close a link between God and the things which he gives, that we identify God with these things and totally forget God in himself, and then if God no longer shows his interest in us by giving us gifts it seems to us that he has abandoned us. For this reason the cross often seems to us a sign of our being abandoned by God. But it can also happen that God does really withdraw himself from our vision in order to prove and strengthen the tenacity of our love for him. Even our Lord Jesus Christ on the cross had this feeling of complete abandonment by God. But even the Lord Jesus never weakened in his love for God.

In reality, God never abandons us in whatever situation we find ourselves. It is possible that he may disappear for a time, for a moment, from our horizon, from our understanding. But the God whom we habitually think of in terms of creation will then appear to us in the true greatness of his glory which is indefinable and inexpressible in human thoughts and words. This is why in the Song of Songs it is said that sometimes God hides himself, and then again reveals himself in a higher and more glorious way:

By night on my bed I sought him whom my soul loveth;
I sought him, but I found him not.
I will rise now, and go about the city in the streets,
and in the broad ways I will seek him whom my soul loveth;
I sought him, but I found him not.

The watchmen that go about the city found me, to whom I said:
Saw ye him whom my soul loveth?

It was but a little that I passed from them,
but I found him whom my soul loveth.
I held him, and would not let him go,
until I had brought him into my mother's house
and into the chamber of her who conceived me.

(Song of Songs 3:1-4)

It is only then that we enter into a relationship with God which is truly personal, a relationship which is above all created things. This relationship with God is one no longer dominated by material images. Our ideas about things and about the gifts which God gives altogether disappear in the light of God himself. Thus purified we give ourselves wholly to God; and we are raised into the dialogue of love exclusively with him. Then we feel that God is infinitely greater than all his gifts and all his creatures, and that in this relationship with him we are raised to a different spiritual level at which we regain in him all that we had lost.

The Christian who has the love of God in him and who thus has love for every person—that love which is an imperishable and inexhaustible reality—feels a greater joy than all the joys which the things of this world can procure, a greater joy than his own existence lived as an isolated individual could ever give him. This is the fact which the righteous discover in their suffering. This cross is given to a man in order that he himself may come to discover God at another level, at an apophatic depth, but also in order to show to other men that there are those who can be attached to God in this way even when all their possessions are taken from them, and even when God himself seems to disappear from their view.

The cross as the mystery of love

The mystery of the cross of the just is the mystery of love between men as eternal persons, the mystery of love for God, and also of the love which above all things must be affirmed amongst men. Truly to love a person means to love them for themselves even when they no longer give us anything, when they no longer seem to have goodwill towards us, even when they seem to show us an incomprehensible coldness or hostility which is altogether contrary to the goodness which they showed to us earlier, even when it seems that the other person has abandoned us even to death. For if we remain firm in our love towards others despite their incomprehensible hardness towards us, we make a true proof of love, of the love which we have for them. This is the love which God himself forms in us and which does indeed raise us from death. When love confronts even death, then it conquers death itself.

He who accepts the death which God gives, with the declaration of love on his lips, gives a supreme proof of a love which will never fail, a love which is given to the person himself and not to his gifts. It is in this supreme love for God that we find the mystery of the cross which is carried by the just, of whom God has given the perfect example in the person of Jesus Christ, and in the earthly suffering which he underwent for the love of God. The Son of God in becoming man accepted the cross first of all to show his love for men, despite their hatred and incomprehension of him which were to be the cause of his death in this world. But then by his death on the cross he has given us the example of a man in whom love for God has resisted to the end, even to being given up to death.

In the case of Job we do not have this picture of a love for God which continues even to death, but we feel that this love could have been there unalterable to the end in Job. All the same, in the beginning Job did not understand the reason for his sufferings which in the end were to be a proof of his love for God. It is Christ who first saw the supreme and absolute value of the cross as a proof of love both of God and of men, love of a worth beyond all else. None the less, Job is the type of Christ, and his second and greater fortune is a type or symbol of the resurrection which the just man who accepts death from God will receive in the end.

Love which does not go so far as the love of Job went or, more clearly, as far as the love of Jesus Christ, is not true love but only conditional, a love conditional on things, that is to say a love of oneself and not a true love of others. It does not reveal the true, infinitely greater worth of persons than of any other created things, nor the eternal basis of their worth in the personal reality of God. In true love a man should transcend himself, go beyond himself, and the supreme act of this transcendence is fulfilled in love for God, who is the Transcendent One.

It is doubtless true and right that persons reveal their love for one another by their gifts, and this is also true in God's relationship with men. In this sense we cannot think of the cross without the world as God's gift. But on the other side we cannot think of the world without the cross. The cross makes this world transparent for God. The cross shows that the world is God's gift, and as such is a lower, and lesser reality than God himself. The cross is the sign of God as a person who is above all his gifts. But it is also the sign of a perfect relationship between God and man. In this sense the cross is specially the sign of the Son of Man in whom this relationship has been perfectly realised. The cross is the sign of the Son of God become man, the sign which he prints on the world by his solidarity with the world.

Without the cross man would be in danger of considering this world as the ultimate reality. Without the cross he would no longer see the world as God's gift. Without the cross the Son of God incarnate would have simply confirmed the image of the world as it is now as the final reality, and strictly speaking he could have been neither God nor God incarnate. The cross completes the fragmentary meaning of this world which has meaning when it is seen as a gift which has its value, but only a relative and not an absolute value. The cross reveals the destiny of the world as it is drawn towards its transfiguration in God by Christ. For this reason at the end of this stage of the world this sign, 'the sign of the Son of Man', will be revealed in the heavens above all the world, as a light, as a meaning, as a destiny which illumines the whole history of man. (Matt. 24:30)

In this way the cross prophetically points to the eschatological, the final destiny of the world. For this reason we associate the sign of the cross with the Holy Trinity, with the Kingdom of God. This is the reason why in the Orthodox Liturgy the cross is printed on the loaf which is used in the Eucharist, bread being at once the sign of God's gift and of man's work, the existential expression of the whole of man's life in this world offered to God. With this sign of the cross the Church blesses, and before all their actions Christians make the sign of the cross in order to dedicate them to God. With this sign the priest blesses the water of Baptism, and also the holy water with which he sprinkles the house, the fields and the whole world in which the Christian lives and works—all is covered with the sign of the cross.

The world has value only in so far as through it we see and receive the revelations and the energies of the person of God who in himself, in his essence, cannot be described, but whose energies are already at work in all creation and will be fully revealed in the transfigured world of the age to come. Until the last day God is at work in this world, leading it towards its resurrection, above all by means of the cross.

Thus the cross is the sign and the means of the salvation of the world. All the world is a gift of God, and by the cross all the world has to be transcended in God. Only in Christ is this meaning of the cross fully revealed. In the cross of Christ the salvation of the world is founded, the salvation of the whole cosmos, because by the cross the tendency of the whole cosmos to transcend itself in God is accomplished. One cannot conceive of a world which is not saved, a world which would always remain in suffering, enclosed in itself, a world in which the cross would not fully fulfil the destiny of the world. Suffering would have no meaning at all unless it was leading the world towards its salvation in God. The hell of an eternal suffering is no longer 'a world', properly speaking, but simply fragments detached from the world without meaning and without solidarity amongst themselves, shadowy, phantasmagoric fragments of the world. In hell suffering is eternal and would finally swallow up the gift. In the kingdom of God the world has been transfigured by the cross through which God himself is finally revealed and glorified.

FAIRACRES PUBLICATIONS
Select list

12	LEARNING TO PRAY Mother Mary Clare	.60
15	DEATH THE GATEWAY TO LIFE Gilbert Shaw	.40
28	JULIAN OF NORWICH A.M. Allchin and SLG	£1.25
43	THE POWER OF THE NAME: The Jesus Prayer in Orthodox Spirituality, Kallistos Ware	£1.25
48	THE WISDOM OF THE DESERT FATHERS, translated with an Introduction by Sr Benedicta Ward SLG	£3.25
55	THEOLOGY AND SPIRITUALITY Andrew Louth	.75
61	KABIR: The Way of Love and Paradox, Sr Rosemary SLG	.75
78	SILENCE IN PRAYER AND ACTION Sr Edmée SLG	.60
84	MYSTERIES OF CHRIST: Extracts from Lucius Cary SSJE	.75
88	CREATIVE SUFFERING Iulia de Beausobre	.75
92	GENTLENESS IN JOHN OF THE CROSS Thomas Kane	.75
94	ST GREGORY NAZIANZEN: SELECTED POEMS, translated with an Introduction by John McGuckin CP	£1.00
95	THE WORLD OF THE DESERT FATHERS, translated with an Introduction by Columba Stewart OSB	£2.25
97	THIS IS THE WORD OF THE LORD Brenda Michael CSCl	.75
107	ROYAL PROGRESS: The Passion of Christ in the Four Evangelists, Sr Stephanie CSD	£1.00
104	GROWING OLD WITH GOD T.N. Rudd	.75
108	THE UNICORN: Meditations on the Love of God, Harry Galbraith Miller	£1.50
111	A KIND OF WATERSHED: An Anglican Lay View of Sacramental Confession, Christine North	£1.25
112	OUT OF THE DEPTHS: Encountering Depression, Gonville ffrench-Beytagh	£1.00
113	THE GLOWING MIND: Prayer in some Caroline Divines, John Byrom	£1.25
114	THE MIND IN THE HEART: Michael Ramsey, Theologian and Man of Prayer, Lorna Kendall	£1.00

A Complete List is available on request; all titles are obtainable, postage extra, from SLG Press, Convent of the Incarnation, Fairacres, Oxford OX4 1TB, England